All Ladybird books are available at most bookshops,
supermarkets and newsagents, or can be ordered direct from:

Ladybird Postal Sales
PO Box 133 Paignton TQ3 2YP England
Telephone: (+44) 01803 554761
Fax: (+44) 01803 663394

A catalogue record for this book is available
from the British Library

Published by Ladybird Books Ltd
A subsidiary of the Penguin Group
A Pearson Company

First published MCMLXXXVIII © Jean and Gareth Adamson
This edition first published MCMXCIX
The moral rights of the author/artist have been asserted

LADYBIRD and the device of a Ladybird are trademarks of
Ladybird Books Ltd Loughborough Leicestershire UK

Topsy + Tim

Little Shoppers

Jean and Gareth Adamson

Ladybird

Early one Saturday morning,
Topsy and Tim and Mummy
and Dad drove to the
supermarket to do their
shopping.

Mummy chose a supermarket
trolley.

"I want to push it," said Topsy.

"I got it first," said Tim.

"Steady on," said Dad. "We'll need two trolleys for all our shopping. You can help me push mine, Topsy."

Mummy had brought a very long shopping list with her. She divided it into two pieces and gave one piece to Dad.

Tim and Mummy went to get some fruit. They got apples, bananas and grapes. Tim chose one orange for himself and one for Topsy.

Dad read his shopping list. "We
need eggs, coffee, cornflakes and
cat food," he said.

Topsy went to find the cat food.
Dad didn't see her go.

Topsy chose Kitty's favourite cat food, then turned and looked for Dad and his trolley – but Dad had disappeared!

Topsy felt lost and lonely and she began to cry. The lady behind the cheese counter looked friendly.

"My mummy and daddy have gone home without me," Topsy told her.

"I'm sure they haven't," said the lady kindly. She looked around and saw a little boy wearing a T-shirt just like Topsy's.

"Is that little boy your brother?" she asked.

"It's Tim!" said Topsy.

Tim took Topsy back to Mummy and Dad.

"Where were you, Topsy?" said Dad.
"I thought I had lost you." He lifted
Topsy up into the child's seat on his
trolley.

"I won't lose you again," he said.

When Tim saw Topsy riding in
Dad's trolley, he wanted a
ride, too.

"Not now, Tim," said Mummy,
"we're nearly at the checkout."

Tim had just spotted the sweets beside the checkout when Mummy said, "I've got a special job for you, Tim. Please will you find two big cardboard boxes to put the shopping in."

Tim found a huge pile of boxes in one corner of the supermarket. He pulled one out from the bottom of the pile. Boxes came tumbling down from the top and one landed on Tim's head.

Topsy laughed when she saw it.
"You look like a spaceman, Tim,"
she said.

Topsy helped Dad to unload the shopping on to the moving counter. The checkout lady added up what it all cost.

Mummy paid for the shopping and she and Tim packed it neatly into the big cardboard boxes, ready to take home.

Dad had one more job for Topsy and Tim to do before they went home. It was to ride in the supermarket helicopter.

Topsy and Tim liked that job best of all!

Topsy is lost. Help her to find her
way back to Dad.

Find the matching T-shirts.

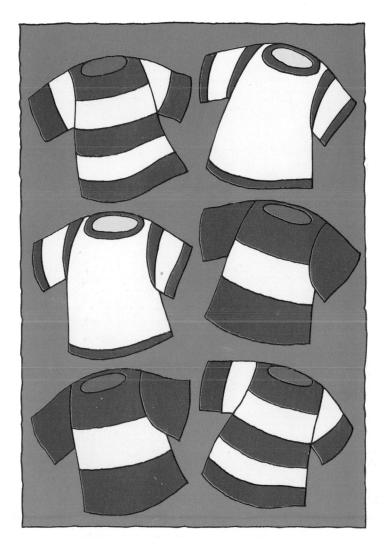

Which trolley is full?
Which is empty?

Whose bag is heavy?
Whose bag is light?

Which slice was cut from the cake?